MW01601673

Draw NEAR

A study of prayer as
presented in the *Catechism*
of the *Catholic Church*

KAREN MAY

All references to the *Catechism of the Catholic Church* will be noted as (CCC #), with the # representing the paragraph being referenced.

All references to Peter Kreeft's *Catholic Christianity, A complete Catechism of the Catholic Beliefs based on the Catechism of the Catholic Church* (Ignatius Press, 2001) will be noted as (Kreeft, p.#)

All Biblical references are taken from the New American translation of the Bible.

Copyright © 2022
Amayzing Graces, LLC
All rights reserved
ISBN: 978-0-9994414-2-8

TABLE OF
contents

Foreword

*"Whether we realize it or not, prayer is the
encounter of God's thirst with ours. God
thirsts that we may thirst for him."*

CCC 2560

The concept of prayer is hard to describe. It is personal, communal, whispered, proclaimed, verbose, silent, eloquent, simple, a quick hello, a deep conversation, and many other things. While the definition of prayer may be simple —Webster defines it as "an address (such as a petition) to God or a god in word or thought"—that simplicity belies a much deeper truth. Prayer is an encounter with God, the Creator of the universe. It is an encounter with Jesus, Savior of the world. It is an encounter with the Holy Spirit, the Spirit of Truth. It is very serious and reverent, focused on lofty and heavenly things, and it is casual and comfortable, barely focused and filled with minor details.

During these next few weeks, we will explore the concept of prayer in the *Catechism*, deepening our understanding of the meaning and practice of prayer. Even more importantly, however, we will take this understanding and use it to help us draw closer to Jesus. We can be scholars of prayer and have no faith, but as intentional practitioners of prayer, our faith and relationship with God will grow.

STUDY FORMAT

This workbook accompanies the *Draw Near* audio series, which is available at **www.AmayzingGraces.com/DrawNear**. Each week, there is a page for you to take notes as you listen to the lesson. If you are doing this study with a group, I recommend that you listen to the lesson during your meeting, pausing the recording for discussion and the sharing of prayer intentions, and returning for the final information and prayer.

GROUP STUDY *(1-1/2 HOUR MEETING)*

1. Listen to the audio recording for the lesson, using the provided space to take notes. *(Approximately 30 minutes)*

2. When indicated in the recording, divide into small groups for discussion. *(30 minutes)*

3. Finish the small group discussion time by sharing prayer intentions and praying for each other. *(15 minutes)*

Each week, as you end your small group discussion time, be sure to pray for each other. You can take turns offering up a prayer and inviting a response with "Lord, hear our prayer," or something similar, or each person can give their request or intention and someone can lead a prayer incorporating them all. There is a page provided for you to note the prayer intentions you want to pray for between meetings. (15 minutes)

4. Return to the large group and share any insights from the small group discussions. *(10 minutes)*

5. Listen to the last part of the audio recording and review the Soul-work assignment for the next week. *(5 minutes)*

NOTE: All *Catechism* references in this workbook refer to the paragraph number in the document, not the page number. You can access the *Catechism* online, or you can purchase your own copy to use with this study.

SOULWORK FORMAT

don't like the idea of homework in a faith study. At its best, homework helps us to deepen our understanding of the lessons we have learned, but at its worst, it is merely busywork. And in reality, very few people do the homework for most Bible studies anyway.

Instead, I will offer you some Soulwork each week. I want you to understand each of the lessons deeply, but more importantly, I want you to be able to put them into practice. This study is not meant for you to learn about prayer, but for you to grow closer to God through a deeper and more vibrant prayer life. I invite and challenge you to start the Soulwork as soon as possible each week. Give yourself time to unwrap the gift waiting for you in each of the activities, and watch for the graces that will surely come from them.

The Soulwork is divided into four days:

- **Pray:** Each week, you will have an opportunity to pray in a specific way. You have learned, you have connected; now go and spend time with God, who can't wait to spend time with you.

- **Reflect:** A great companion to this study is Peter Kreeft's *Catholic Christianity*. The Reflect section contains a quote related to the Catechism teachings that you have learned about, connected with, and prayed with. They are beautiful and deeply meaningful. Spend some time (maybe in prayer!) meditating on what he says.

- **Engage:** To prepare for the next lesson, you will read a section of the Catechism. These questions will help you get more out of your reading, and prepare you for the lesson and discussion during the class.

- **Connect:** Now that you have read the paragraphs from the Catechism, how will you put them into practice? These questions direct you to a deeper understanding and a more meaningful practice of the aspects of prayer that you have just learned.

I am so excited to share these lessons with you. I pray that through them you are drawn closer to God, and that you see how close God is to you. You are in my prayers.

LISTEN TO THE INTRODUCTION
Talk Notes

DISCUSSION QUESTIONS FOR INTRODUCTION

1. What do you hope to get out of this class?

   _____

   _____

2. How content are you with your prayer life right now?

   _____

   _____

3. How would you describe your prayer life in general?

   _____

   _____

4. What is your most comfortable mode, type, and/or location for prayer?

   _____

   _____

PRAYER INTENTIONS

Write down your own prayer intentions and those of your group here and pray for them during the next week. The power of prayer is only seen when we pay attention to what we are praying for.

_____

_____

_____

LESSON ONE

Prayer in the
Old Testament

Soulwork

DAY 1: PRAY

(Each week we will start with an invitation to pray in a way that is related to the talk that you just heard. Try to do this the day of or the day after the class each week so you have plenty of time to put your new understandings of prayer into practice)

- Find a place that you want to pray this week. Don't worry about decorating it or if there are enough holy items around. Just make it comfortable, away from distractions, and easy to get to.

- Use the next page to journal your prayers if you would like, and spend some time regularly each day this week in prayer, even if it's only five minutes each day. Pray from your heart.

- What do you want? What do you need?

- Give praise or thanksgiving.

- Give space and time for God to respond to you.

prayer journal

_____

_____

_____

_____

_____

_____

_____

_____

_____

_____

_____

_____

_____

_____

_____

_____

_____

_____

_____

Soulwork

DAY 2: REFLECT

"We know God better by one moment of prayer - of praise or thanks or contrition - than by a thousand books. When we only talk about him, we only know about him; when we talk to him, we get to know him."
(Peter Kreeft, Catholic Christianity, p. 376)

reflection notes

_____

_____

_____

_____

_____

_____

_____

_____

_____

_____

$\mathscr{Soulwork}$

DAY 3: ENGAGE

Read paragraphs 2566-2597 of the *Catechism of the Catholic Church*.

1. Paragraph 2569 talks about prayer as "walking with God." When have you felt like God was present in something you were experiencing?

_____

_____

_____

2. Moses learns how to pray through his dialogue with God. "He balks, makes excuses, above all questions.: (CCC 2575) How is your prayer a dialogue with God? How is it not?

_____

_____

_____

3. In paragraph 2581, the Temple is described as the place for the education of the people in prayer. However, "ritualism often encouraged an excessively external worship." How are you tempted to an external form of worship? What rituals help you to focus on an interior worship that connects your heart with God?

_____

_____

_____

Soulwork

DAY 4: CONNECT

Read paragraphs 2566-2597 of the *Catechism of the Catholic Church*.

1. What are your methods of prayer right now? (i.e., words, deeds, intercession, contemplation) There may be several different types.

_____

_____

_____

2. Pray with Psalm 51. How is God speaking to your heart? What are you holding back? Can you offer it now?

_____

_____

_____

3. Reflect on how the prayers of the Psalms express and acclaim the work of God. (CCC 2587) Use this space to express and acclaim the work of God that you see in your life and in the world.

_____

_____

_____

LISTEN TO LESSON ONE:
PRAYER IN THE OLD TESTAMENT

Talk Notes

_____

_____

_____

_____

_____

_____

_____

_____

_____

_____

_____

_____

_____

_____

_____

_____

_____

PRAYER INTENTIONS

Write down your own prayer intentions and those of your group here and pray for them during the next week. The power of prayer is only seen when we pay attention to what we are praying for.

_____

_____

_____

_____

_____

_____

LESSON TWO

Jesus and the Church

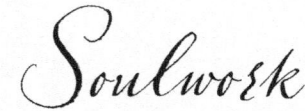

Soulwork

DAY 1: PRAY

This week, we learned that the Book of Psalms is a book of prayer that expresses almost every emotion we can feel.

I invite you to pray with the Psalms this week. Choose one to pray all week or choose a different one each day. Let them help you to say what you are feeling. Here are some suggestions:

- Suffering - Psalm 40
- Doubt - Psalm 77
- Joy - Psalm 148
- Awe/Wonder - Psalm 139
- Hope - Psalm 27
- Praise - Psalm 96
- Waiting - Psalm 43
- Fear - Psalm 121

prayer journal

_____

_____

_____

_____

_____

_____

_____

_____

_____

DAY 2: REFLECT

So our motive for praying, our right answer to the question "Why should I pray?" is first of all: "Because God wants it." We need it, but that is why God wants it.
(Kreeft, p. 377)

reflection notes

DAY 3: ENGAGE

Read paragraphs 2598-2649 of the *Catechism of the Catholic Church.*

1. How does the way Jesus prayed inspire your prayer? (CCC 2599-2604)

    _____

    _____

    _____

2. The Church's prayer is "founded on apostolic faith; authenticated by charity; [and] nourished in the Eucharist." (CCC 2624) Does this describe your prayer? If so, how does that affect your prayer? If not, what is missing?

    _____

    _____

    _____

3. We can only give to God that which God has given to us. (CCC 2645) How does that statement change your understanding of praise, forgiveness, tithing, etc.?

    _____

    _____

    _____

DAY 4: CONNECT

Read paragraphs 2598-2649 of the *Catechism of the Catholic Church.*

1. What praise can you give God today?

    _____

    _____

    _____

2. The *Catechism* tells us we should give thanks before we receive a gift. (CCC 2604) How can you do this in your own prayer? Does it help you to put your request in its proper place?

    _____

    _____

    _____

3. The Eucharist contains and expresses all forms of prayer. (CCC 2643) How does it contain and express adoration, praise, thanksgiving, intercession, and petition?

    _____

    _____

    _____

LISTEN TO LESSON TWO:
JESUS AND THE CHURCH

Talk Notes

_____

_____

_____

_____

_____

_____

_____

_____

_____

_____

_____

_____

PRAYER INTENTIONS

Write down your own prayer intentions and those of your group here and pray for them during the next week. The power of prayer is only seen when we pay attention to what we are praying for.

_____

_____

_____

_____

_____

_____

_____

LESSON THREE

Traditions of Prayer

Soulwork

DAY 1: PRAY

In our New Testament focus this week, we heard about some pretty powerful ways to pray. One of the gifts of Mary's "Yes" to the Angel Gabriel is her prayer of praise in response to the call she has received.

- Today, pray with Mary's Magnificat in Luke 1:46-55.

- I invite you to start your prayers this week with praise and adoration - every time.

prayer journal

_____

_____

_____

_____

_____

_____

_____

_____

_____

DAY 2: REFLECT

We must begin with God rather than self because "that's the way it is", that is the way reality is ordered. God is first, and to treat him as second or as a means to our ends is to reverse reality's order and to have a false God, an idol; and all idols break.
(Kreeft, p. 381)

reflection notes

_____

_____

_____

_____

_____

_____

_____

_____

_____

DAY 3: ENGAGE

Read paragraphs 2650-2696 of the *Catechism of the Catholic Church*.

1. The *Catechism* speaks of "several wellsprings where Christ awaits us to enable us to drink of the Holy Spirit." (CCC 2652) These include the Word of God, the liturgy of the Church, virtues of faith, hope, and charity, and our every day. What wellspring(s) do you drink from?

   _____

   _____

   _____

2. Who in the Trinity do you primarily pray to/relate to? God the Father, Jesus the Son, or the Holy Spirit? Has this changed over the years? Are you drawn to grow in prayer with another person of the Trinity?

   _____

   _____

   _____

3. How did you learn to pray?

   _____

   _____

   _____

DAY 4: CONNECT

Read paragraphs 2650-2696 of the *Catechism of the Catholic Church.*

4. What is your prayer life like now? Has it changed since you started this class? How?

    _____

    _____

    _____

5. Do you have a devotion to Mary? Why or why not? How do you see her leading people to her son, Jesus? (In prayer, in scripture, in your life)

    _____

    _____

    _____

6. Do you have favorite Saints? When do you tend to ask for their intercession?

    _____

    _____

    _____

LISTEN TO LESSON THREE:
TRADITIONS OF PRAYER

Talk Notes

_____

_____

_____

_____

_____

_____

_____

_____

_____

_____

_____

_____

_____

PRAYER INTENTIONS

Write down your own prayer intentions and those of your group here and pray for them during the next week. The power of prayer is only seen when we pay attention to what we are praying for.

_____

_____

_____

_____

_____

_____

_____

LESSON FOUR

Types of Prayer

Soulwork

DAY 1: PRAY

This week we learned about several prayer practices we have to help us pray, and one of them is memorized or rote prayer.

- It is important to savor the meaning of memorized prayers rather than just reciting them. (CCC 2688) Pray a memorized or rote prayer you know in a deliberate way, contemplating each phrase before moving to the next.

- Some examples are the Our Father, Hail Mary, the Memorare, Come, Holy Spirit, St. Francis prayer, Litany of Humility.

prayer journal

_____

_____

_____

_____

_____

_____

_____

_____

DAY 2: REFLECT

Do we need set prayers at all? Should we not just be spontaneous and use our own words instead of words composed by others?

We should do both. As we need other people's works, we need their words–as in music and in literature, so in prayer. It is as natural to pray others' prayers as to sing others' songs. For when we do, we make them our own.
(Kreeft, p. 384)

reflection notes

_____

_____

_____

_____

_____

_____

_____

_____

_____

DAY 3: ENGAGE

Read paragraphs 2697-2724 of the *Catechism of the Catholic Church.*

1. What is the rhythm of your prayer life? (CCC 2698)

   _____

   _____

   _____

2. Have you been to adoration? If so, why do you go? What is the experience like? If not, why don't you go? What is getting in the way?

   _____

   _____

   _____

3. Which type of prayer do you use most often? Which type is the most impactful for you?

   _____

   _____

   _____

DAY 4: CONNECT

Read paragraphs 2697-2724 of the *Catechism of the Catholic Church*.

1. "In praying, do not babble like the pagans, who think that they will be heard because of their many words." (Matthew 6:7) Do we have to be brief in our vocal prayers? How do you pray vocally (internally or externally) and avoid what Jesus is warning of in this passage?

    _____

    _____

    _____

2. One of the sources for prayerful meditation is history - "the page on which the 'today' of God is written." (CCC 2705) Where do you see God when you meditate on recent or past history?

    _____

    _____

    _____

3. Have you ever sat in silence before God as you pray? What are some of the challenges to silent contemplation for you? What draws you to that silence?

    _____

    _____

    _____

LISTEN TO LESSON FOUR: TYPES OF PRAYER

Talk Notes

PRAYER INTENTIONS

Write down your own prayer intentions and those of your group here and pray for them during the next week. The power of prayer is only seen when we pay attention to what we are praying for.

_____

_____

_____

_____

_____

_____

_____

LESSON FIVE

Difficulties in Prayer

Soulwork

DAY 1: PRAY

The three types of prayer we heard about this week are vocal prayer, meditative prayer, and contemplative prayer. This week, I invite you to be intentional about the type of prayer that you are using.

Go to adoration at least once this week. Better yet, go three times, and focus on a different prayer type each time - vocal, meditative, and contemplative.

prayer journal

_____

_____

_____

_____

_____

_____

_____

_____

_____

_____

Soulwork

DAY 2: REFLECT

*In contemplative prayer there is a forgetting of self-aware-
ness and a renunciation of self-will. What replaces self is not
nothingness but Jesus. "This focus on Jesus is a renunciation
of self" (CCC 2715)–not of the reality of the self (it is not an
illusion) or the value of the self (it is the image of God), but
of its habitual turning-in-on-itself, a renunciation of self-con-
sciousness and self-will. It is a training for and a foretaste of
our future heavenly "ecstasy" (the word means "standing-out-
side-yourself"), for it is a sharing in the very life of God.*
(Kreeft, p. 387)

reflection notes

_____

_____

_____

_____

_____

_____

_____

_____

DAY 3: ENGAGE

Read paragraphs 2725-2758 of the *Catechism of the Catholic Church*.

1. Reflect on the sentence "We pray as we live, because we live as we pray." (CCC 2725) How have you experienced this in your life?

   _____

   _____

   _____

2. Our distractions in prayer reveal what we are attached to (CCC 2729). What do your distractions and obstacles to prayer say about what you are attached to? Do you think the cure to distraction is as simple as turning your heart back to Jesus? Try it.

   _____

   _____

   _____

3. How do you respond when your prayers are answered? What do you do when you feel like they aren't being heard?

   _____

   _____

   _____

DAY 4: CONNECT

Read paragraphs 2725-2758 of the *Catechism of the Catholic Church.*

1. What image of God is motivating your prayer right now? (CCC 2735) How can you adjust your prayers to incorporate the image of God as the Father of our Lord Jesus Christ instead of seeing God as an instrument to be used?

   _____

   _____

   _____

2. What is God waiting for you to ask Him in prayer? (CCC 2736) Can you ask Him here?

   _____

   _____

   _____

3. To pray unceasingly is to invite Jesus into everything we do – praying through our thoughts, our words, and our actions. How are you being called to incorporate prayer more into your life?

   _____

   _____

   _____

LISTEN TO LESSON FIVE: DIFFICULTIES IN PRAYER

Talk Notes

_____

_____

_____

_____

_____

_____

_____

_____

_____

_____

_____

_____

_____

PRAYER INTENTIONS

Write down your own prayer intentions and those of your group here and pray for them during the next week. The power of prayer is only seen when we pay attention to what we are praying for.

_____

_____

_____

_____

_____

_____

Conclusion

Conclusion

Now that our study is finished, I leave you with a final invitation to pray, a reflection, and a chance to see how your faith and prayer life have grown. Thank you for joining me for this study. I hope it has inspired you and encouraged you in your faith, but most of all I pray that it has helped you draw closer to God than you even thought was possible.

You have just begun the most beautiful journey. I encourage you to keep going. Keep praying, keep exploring, keep sharing your prayers with each other. God is reaching for you. Keep reaching back!

Soulwork

DAY 1: PRAY

What difficulties are you having with prayer? Bring them to prayer, asking for the grace to overcome them. Be honest and open, and then spend some time listening and waiting for a response. Don't worry if you don't get one, just create the space. It will fill the rest of your day.

prayer journal

_____
_____
_____
_____
_____
_____
_____
_____
_____
_____
_____
_____
_____
_____
_____
_____
_____
_____
_____

DAY 2: REFLECT

Finally, God waits with his answer in order to make us "pray without ceasing." "This tireless fervor can come only from love: (CCC2742). It is to elicit our love that God does everything he does. He does not need us to love him, but we do. So he plunges us into the fire of battle in order to plunge us more deeply into the fire of love. The battle is within us, not between us and God, it is a battle of love against its enemies. "Against our dullness and laziness, the battle of prayer is that of humble, trusting, and persevering love" (CCC 2742). Love with these three qualities is a gift of God and the most precious gift in life.
(Kreeft, p. 390)

reflection notes

_____

_____

_____

_____

_____

_____

_____

_____

_____

PERSONAL REVIEW

1. What are some of the insights, resources, practices, and/or blessings you have gotten from this class?

   _____

   _____

   _____

2. How content are you with your prayer life now that you have finished this study?

   _____

   _____

   _____

3. How has your prayer life evolved during this study?

   _____

   _____

   _____

4. Has there been a change in the way you feel most comfortable praying?

   _____

   _____

   _____

Link to Audio Lessons:

www.AmayzingGraces.com/DrawNear

NOTE: All *Catechism* references in this workbook refer to the paragraph number in the document, not the page number. You can access the *Catechism* online, or you can purchase your own copy to use with this study.

Made in the USA
Monee, IL
12 June 2025

18985518R00033